THE
FINAL ACT
OF
KINDNESS

Published by Mynd Matters Publishing
715 Peachtree Street NE
Suites 100 & 200
Atlanta, GA 30308
www.myndmatterspublishing.com

978-1-957092-13-3 (pbk)
978-1-957092-14-0 (hcv)
978-1-957092-15-7 (ebk)

FIRST EDITION

THE
FINAL ACT
OF
KINDNESS

PREPARING FINANCIALLY FOR THE INEVITABLE

CYNTHIA VAIL LOWE

Dedicated to the victims and their families who lost their lives during the Covid-19 pandemic.

CONTENTS

INTRODUCTION

The Final Act of Kindness is a wellness guide to ensure your family's estate is in order. Not simply as an afterthought once you've left this earth but as a proactive plan created while you are still alive. My aim is to help others avoid the pain, confusion, and frustration that often occurs for surviving family members when someone dies without an estate plan. You shouldn't have to "put your hands in a fire to know you will burn."

I am not an attorney. However, the experience I've garnered does give me some level of proficiency on this topic as I've experienced the death of nearly every category of family member. I also work with a team of attorneys and experts in income protection to ensure I have a holistic understanding of these matters.

Knowing what documents you should complete to protect your family is only one of the benefits of this handbook. It also includes practical suggestions to assist you and your loved ones, not only after you have transitioned but if you become homebound or are incapable of taking care of your affairs while alive. Included are samples and definitions of legal documents and information to help lessen some of the stress your loved ones must face when you are gone. This frees you to live in your "power of now" and not worry about the future as protections are in place.

In Oprah Winfrey's, *What I Know For Sure*, she states, "The gift of deciding to face your mortality without turning away or flinching is the gift of recognizing that because you will die, you must live now. Whether you flounder or flourish is always in your hands—you are the biggest influence in your life. Your journey began with a choice, to get up, step out and live fully."

MY STORY

I was a successful employee with the city of New York and was promoted to progressively increased responsibilities over the span of forty-one years. I was married to a loving, supportive husband and we were blessed to have a daughter who was the apple of her father's eye. We worshiped at a neighborhood church and traveled when time allowed. Life was fantastic.

All that changed on Sunday, February 13, 1994. Instead of going to church, we decided to spend a day at home together. Since so many things on television were a bit too explicit for our liking, we often watched sports together. While my daughter and husband were watching college basketball, I was in the kitchen cooking my husband's favorite meal, barbeque spareribs, collard greens and potato salad. As I was cooking, Angela came into the kitchen and said, "Mommy, something is wrong with Daddy." I swiftly went to my husband's side and found him unresponsive. I called 911 and proceeded to perform mouth to mouth resuscitation. I breathed into my husband's mouth, waited—one, two, three—and breathed into his mouth again before repeating the steps. Once the ambulance arrived, they quickly put him on a gurney took him to the hospital. By the end of that day, I was a widow and a single parent. I never envisioned I would be either.

My husband and I did not have a will. We had life insurance, but it was insufficient to substitute for the lost income my husband contributed to the household. Our daughter was nine years old at the time and I had at least thirteen more years to financially support her.

I found a second life insurance policy that I thought had lapsed. Since we never collected the dividends, the policy was still in effect. Unfortunately, I was not the beneficiary. My husband's deceased mother was. I contacted the life insurance company to submit my mother-in-love's death certificate and my marriage license so I could collect the proceeds from the policy. Wrong! My living father-in-law was the relative next in line to collect the policy. He wrote a letter disavowing his claim to the policy and I was sure all obstacles were removed from my collecting the policy as his widow. Guess what? I still was not next in line to collect the money. My daughter was the beneficiary as she is a blood relative. The next step in this process in New York City was as follows:

1. I, her mother, who awakened during a C-section to birth her, had to apply to become her *legal* guardian in New York State Surrogate Court.
2. The money resulting from the insurance policy had to be placed in a passbook savings account instead of a higher interest paying certificate of deposit.
3. To add insult to injury, when I applied to use some of the resources for my daughter's tuition, the judge denied the request. He told me that no one forced me to keep my daughter in private school.

Imagine my frustration and sadness. The next issue we faced was changing the co-op apartment we lived in to my name. I did not know the process to obtain Letters of Administration. The co-op board was of no assistance. Thank God for a neighbor who led me through the process.

My story communicates many things but ultimately, it emphasizes the need for estate planning. Death is no respecter of a person's age. My husband and I were in our early forties when he passed. Have the courage to initiate an uncomfortable conversation that protects those you hold most dear.

Now, let me ask you some questions. Did I know my husband would die the day he did? Do we get advance notice of death? Can we prepare for death? If so, how?

COMPLETE A FINAL ACT OF KINDNESS!

So far, in the United States, more than 80 million people have contracted the coronavirus with almost one million of those cases resulting in death. How many of the 80 million have set up a *Final Act of Kindness?*

Two of the people diagnosed with COVID-19 were Ernestine and Julian Brown. They were married for over fifty years. Mr. and Mrs. Brown cared about what would happen to each other when they transitioned. They set up their Estate Plan.

In the beginning stages of the pandemic, they were victims of the coronavirus. To lessen the distress on their bodies from this disease, they both were placed on a respirator and induced into a coma. Because their daughter did not know the location of their essential documents, Mrs. Brown had to be awakened so her daughter could find out where the needed documents were located. At the same time, she was informed that the love of her life, her partner for more than fifty years, had succumbed to this terrible disease.

Location, location, location is everything. Please inform someone of the location of your documents. The location of important documents must be shared with a loved one. Keeping the whereabouts of these documents a secret does not help your family during a time when they are most vulnerable.

The Final Act of Kindness includes taking the legal actions needed to provide clarity, guidance, and security for those you will leave behind upon your death. Laws regarding estate planning vary in each state. An attorney in your state of residence who specializes in Estate Planning is an expert at completing these forms and gives you the best advice for your financial situation. You should consult with one of them. The forms listed below are the essential documents for a basic estate plan. The definitions are according to New York state but are similar to other states.

- Power of Attorney
- Living Will
- Health Care Proxy—Organ Donations
- Will–remember to name a guardian for minor children
- Revocable Trust with a disability clause

In addition to completing and filing legal documents, there is other information that will assist your family during their time of bereavement. A vital list of things to consider is included in this guide along with a checklist and space for you to include your specific details. Use this book to create your *Final Act of Kindness* for your loved ones.

THE GRIEVING PROCESS

Grieving is a personal process. No one can tell you how long it takes to grieve. I suggest everyone go to grief counseling. It took me ten years to seek help. I will always remember the loss of my loved ones, but I now have tools to help me ease the pain of not having them. When my husband first died, I knew I had a child to raise and she did not need to lose both parents. Now I am living for me. I've realized that out of the worst tragedies, blessings occur. *The Final Act Of Kindness* is the blessing I received. My prayer is that it is a blessing for you as well.

Grief – a universal human experience. At one time or another, we all will experience the loss of someone. At one time or another, we all will transition from earth. How we and our loved ones cope with death is personal and unique. No one can define how long grief will last or predict the length of time it will take to go through each stage of grief. It is helpful to have a support system during this time. A support system can consist of anyone you feel comfortable with (I.e., family members, friends, religious family, pastors, rabbis, imams as well as professional counseling). Remember, you or your loved ones don't have to travel this difficult journey alone even though sometimes you might want to.

Denial – In order to protect yourself from the shock of hearing of a loved one's passing, your first response may be to deny that the situation has occurred. Facing the reality that a loved one died is very painful. It is important not to ignore the pain. Feeling the pain and not masking it with the use of artificial substances like drugs and alcohol is the best way to proceed.

Anger – Many will find themselves angry at the world during this time.

Frustration might cause you to have anger issues. Those who are close relatives, those who still have their loved ones, and/or whomever you respect as your God, are prime targets for your anger.

Bargaining – During this time, you promise that if your loved one comes back, you will become the most perfect individual that ever existed. You will always love them and won't fuss, fight, or argue. You also examine the steps you might have taken to save your loved one.

Depression – When a loved one passes, it is natural to feel the worst type of sadness you have ever experienced. During the stage of depression, you will likely withdraw from normal activities and feel as if you are in a fog of sadness. You may find it difficult to go on without that person in your life. This is a stage of grief when you need your support system around you most. If you start to feel overwhelmed, seek professional help as an option.

Acceptance – When we lose a loved one, they can never be replaced. We make new relationships, but we don't forget our loved ones. There is no betrayal to the lost loved one when we start to live life again and enjoy it. We must learn to reestablish roles by either giving them to others or taking them on ourselves.

THE FINAL ACT OF KINDNESS

HEALTH PROXY

I was on my way to eat breakfast on a Saturday afternoon when my phone rang. One of my best friends had passed away. I had just left the hospital. She died so quickly. I was happy I got to tell her goodbye. We had been friends for over fifty years. Out of all the people I had ever given advice to about *The Final Act of Kindness*, she followed every step. What I did not know to tell her was to inform all her children and grandchildren about her final wishes. She did not want her life to continue artificially. Murderer was what her child was called for following the wishes in her mother's health proxy. Have the conversation with immediate family members so this does not happen to the person who is carry out your wishes.

The New York Health Care Proxy Law allows you to appoint someone you trust (the who), for example, a family member or close friend to make health care decisions for you if you lose the ability to make decisions for yourself. By appointing a health care agent, you can make sure that health care providers follow your wishes. Your agent can also decide how your wishes apply as your medical condition changes. Hospitals, doctors, and other health care providers must follow your agent's decisions as if they were your own. You may give the person you select as your health care agent as little or as much authority as you want. You may allow your agent to make all health care decisions or only certain ones. You may also give your agent instructions that he or she follows. This form can also be used to document your wishes or instructions for organ and/or tissue donation.

LIVING WILL

A Living Will is a written document that allows a patient to give explicit instructions about medical treatment to be administered when the patient is terminally ill or permanently unconscious and is also called an advance directive.

With improvements in modern medicine, the life of persons who are terminally ill or permanently unconscious can be prolonged. For increasing numbers of persons, the decision of whether to prolong life is made in the form of a written document called a living will. The living will is one type of advance directive that may be used by a person before incapacitation to outline a full range of treatment preferences or, most often, to reject treatment.

A living will extends the principle of consent, whereby patients must agree to any medical intervention before doctors can proceed. It allows the patient to guide health care for the future when she may be too ill to make decisions concerning care. It can be revoked by the patient at any time. For many, the living will preserves personal control and eases the decision-making burden of a family.

Forty-two states and the District of Columbia have living-will statutes that make a properly executed living will legally binding. In states that do not have a statute, living wills stand as a clear expression of the patient's wishes. Living-will statutes require that the person be legally competent to execute the will and that they will be witnessed by at least one disinterested person. Once a person who has a valid living will is terminally ill, the attending physician and a second physician must certify in writing that there is no reasonable expectation for improvement in the patient's condition and that death will occur because of the incurable disease, illness, or injury.

Upon this certification, the doctor is obligated to follow the instructions contained in the living will. This typically means the patient does not want any medical procedures that serve only to prolong, but not prevent, the dying process. Therefore, if the patient is unable to breathe, the doctor is not required to connect the patient to a respirator. A patient may state in a living will that he does not want a feeding tube if unable to swallow food. Another common directive is to forbid resuscitation if the patient's heart stops beating.

Living wills have been criticized because they are usually limited to the withholding or withdrawing of life-sustaining procedures from a patient with a terminal condition or terminal illness, and thus do not accurately reflect the broad legal right to refuse treatment. In addition, by their very nature, living wills reduce the patient's wishes to writing, and thus may be too rigid (or too vague) to adapt to changing interests or anticipate future circumstances.

To overcome these problems, many states have enacted statutes that permit a competent adult to designate a surrogate decision maker (also termed: a health care proxy or agent) to make health care decisions for her in the event of incapacitation. The proxy's authority is usually not limited to decisions about life-sustaining treatment. A proxy can supplement a living will.

All fifty states have durable-power-of-attorney statutes that permit an individual (the principal) to designate another person (the attorney in fact) to perform specific tasks during any period of incapacity. Though most of these statutes do not expressly refer to medical care decisions, no court has ruled that they preclude the delegation of medical decision-making authority to the attorney in fact.

LAST WILL AND TESTAMENT

A will can protect your assets and help minimize the chances of a fight over the distribution of your estate. The most important thing a will accomplishes is that it allows you to make decisions about your assets and not someone else. If you die without a will, your estate may not be distributed as you would prefer.

A will can do the following:

- Provide for your family
- Specify whom you would like to receive your property
- State your funeral and burial instructions
- Create a trust for minor children
- Disinherit a person(s)
- Name a guardian for minor children

REVOCABLE TRUST

I suggest you enlist the services of an attorney for a Revocable Trust. Establishing a Revocable Trust is considerably more expensive than establishing a will. You will make the decision to have both or one. A Revocable Trust allows you to place assets in the trust and when you die, your beneficiaries do not go to probate court to obtain the assets. The person or people benefiting from the trust are the beneficiaries. Because a revocable trust can list one or more beneficiaries, the trust avoids probate, which is the legal process of distributing assets of a will. Having a Revocable Trust does not mean you should not have a will. A trust does not keep you from paying taxes.

POWER OF ATTORNEY (POA)

Harry was retired and lived alone in his house. He was a widower of many years. He enjoyed his independence and loved his children and grandchildren. When his son called to find out why Harry did not meet him for their regularly scheduled Saturday brunch date, he was concerned when Harry did not answer the home or house phones. Imagine the horror he faced upon discovering his dad paralyzed on the floor of the bathroom. Eventually going to a rehabilitation home after suffering a stroke, Harry was unable to take care of his financial business. Harry implemented a durable Power of Attorney after his wife passed, allowing his trusted son to become his agent. Harry recovered but his son continued to act on his dad's behalf.

There are two types of POAs. An ordinary Power of Attorney is only valid if you can manage your own affairs. It becomes invalid when you lose the ability to make decisions concerning your life. A durable Power of Attorney, if created before you lose the capacity to make decisions concerning your life, will remain valid even after this capacity is lost. If you want your representative to make decisions for you after you have lost the ability to make decisions for yourself, then you should choose durable.

Caution: A durable power of attorney is an important document. It gives the person whom you designate (your "Agent") broad powers to handle your property during your lifetime, which may include powers to mortgage, sell, or otherwise dispose of any real or personal property without advance notice to you or approval by you. These powers will continue to exist even after you become disabled or incompetent. These powers are explained more fully in your state's law.

A Power of Attorney contract does not authorize anyone to make medical or other health care decisions. You may execute a health care proxy to do this. If there is anything about this form that you do not understand, you should ask a lawyer to explain it to you.

IMPORTANT INFORMATION

Gone are the days of passbook savings accounts. In this world of technological advances, more business and social activity is being conducted via the Internet. To have an account online, one must have a password and or a User ID. Leaving a list of this information will assist loved ones in protecting your estate.

By completing your *Final Act of Kindness*, you are providing guidance and clarity for your loved ones as well as preparing them for the inevitable. The following pages include considerations and vital information to help them navigate legal and financial matters in your absence.

PEOPLE TO CONTACT

Pastor/Spiritual Leader – Offer comfort and support for gathered family and friends. To participate in the funeral or homegoing service. This person might also have to sign the death certificate.

Estate Lawyer – Help the executor navigate the process of paying final bills, providing clarity on the will, taking the will through probate, etc.

Executor of Your Estate – Manage the decedent's assets including closing out credit accounts, paying bills, coordinating clothing/goods from a residence, as well as selling a property or transfer ownership to the heirs.

Family and Friends – A list of the names and phone numbers for the executor (or those helping to disseminate the news) to contact. While we have some space included in this guidebook for the initial group of contacts, consider drafting a detailed list and clearly marking the file on your computer or in your cellphone notes. You can also list the file name in that section of this guidebook to provide more clarity. *Note: someone must be able to access your phone or computer.*

Undertaker – Designates funeral home that prepares you for homegoing service. Loved ones should request a minimum of 10 death certificates. A copy or an original will be needed to close accounts and obtain assets that belong to the deceased.

Life Insurance Company – Will distribute the payout to your estate. Your name, SSN, policy number, and a death certificate will be needed. If you do not have life insurance, which you should, list the details for your burial fund.

Landlord – Will provide access to retrieve your personal belongings and prepare the residence for new tenants. If you rent, make sure any family members that live with you are listed on your lease or known via affidavit to the landlords.

Bank(s) and Investment Companies – Secure financial accounts. The executor must submit a death certificate to start the distribution of assets to listed beneficiaries.

Safe Deposit Box – Provide the location of the key, address of the box, and pertinent information needed to enter the safety deposit box.

Subscription Services – Includes newspapers, magazines, streaming services, etc. Provide details to help loved ones cancel existing subscriptions.

USPS/Mail – Forward mail to the address of the relative (or agent) working with the attorney and executor of your estate.

Social Security Office *(if applicable)* – Contact and notify to stop the disbursement of checks.

Pension *(if applicable)* – Contact and notify to stop the disbursement of checks and have beneficiary forms sent.

Service Providers (cellphone, home phone, internet, cable, etc.) – Executor must contact these entities to cancel accounts.

Jewelry, Clothes, Personal Items – Designate any special items to family and friends that may appreciate receiving them. List this information in detail and consider also discussing the list with your estate attorney and/or executor so your wishes will be followed.

Holidays – If you were the person who always prepared special holiday dinners or organized gatherings, start the conversation with someone who you believe will want to continue this and other family traditions.

SPECIAL NOTE

Make time to write a letter to your spouse, significant other, children, parents and/or friends. While it may not be easy, your words may help console them during their time of bereavement.

MY FINAL ACT OF KINDNESS

CHECKLIST

Full Legal Name _____

Home Address _____

_____

_____

P.O. Box _____
(location and number)

_____

Safe Deposit Box _____
(location and number)

Social Security Number (SSN) _____

LOG-IN & ACCESS INFORMATION
Usernames and passwords

Computer(s):

_____

_____

Cellphone(s):

_____

_____

Email(s):

_____

_____

_____

DESIGNATIONS & KEY CONTACTS

	Name	*Phone Number*
Executor of Estate		
Estate Attorney		
Pastor/Spiritual Leader		
Manager/Work Contact		
Landlord		
Community Doctor		
Military Leadership		
Undertaker/Funeral Home		
Social Security Office		

FAMILY & FRIENDS TO CONTACT

Name   *Relationship*   *Phone Number*

_____

_____

_____

_____

_____

_____

INSURANCE

Life Insurance

Company _____ Policy # _____

Company _____ Policy # _____

Company _____ Policy # _____

Health Insurance

Company _____ Policy # _____

Dental Insurance

Company _____ Policy # _____

Vision Insurance

Company _____ Policy # _____

Other Insurance

Company _____ Policy # _____

Burial Fund Details *(if applicable):*

BANKING & INVESTMENTS

Financial Planner/Investment Advisor

Name _____

Phone Number _____

Email Address _____

Savings Account(s)
Bank Name(s)/Phone Number(s)/Account Number(s)

_____

_____

Checking Account(s)
Bank Name(s)/Phone Number(s)/Account Number(s)

_____

_____

_____

Investment Account(s)
Bank Name(s)/Phone Number(s)/Account Number(s)

_____

_____

_____

AUTOMOBILES

Car #1

Make/Model _____ VIN #_____

    ☐ I Own my car (with no debt)

    ☐ I Own my car (with debt)

    ☐ I Lease my car   Details: _____

Car #2

Make/Model _____ VIN #_____

    ☐ I Own my car (with no debt)

    ☐ I Own my car (with debt)

    ☐ I Lease my car   Details: _____

Car #3

Make/Model _____ VIN #_____

    ☐ I Own my car (with no debt)

    ☐ I Own my car (with debt)

    ☐ I Lease my car   Details: _____

CREDIT CARDS

Card Name/Type	Account #	Phone Number
_____	_____	_____
_____	_____	_____
_____	_____	_____
_____	_____	_____
_____	_____	_____

SUBSCRIPTIONS

Company/Brand   Account #

Magazine(s) _____

_____

_____

Newspaper(s) _____

_____

_____

TV/Digital Streaming Platform(s):

_____

_____

_____

Apps:

_____

_____

_____

SOCIAL MEDIA

Social Media Platform   Username & Password

_____   _____

_____   _____

_____   _____

_____   _____

_____   _____

MISCELLANEOUS INFORMATION

_____

_____

_____

_____

_____

_____

FUNERAL PREPARATIONS

There are many questions to answer regarding your funeral or homegoing service. The cost and location may be first to come to mind but there are many additional details to consider in your plan. People often struggle to make decisions about funeral or homegoing services for a loved one unless they've had a conversation about that person's wishes and wants.

Have you given any thought to your funeral? What preferences do you have about your service? Have you discussed your preferences with family members? Part of your *Final Act of Kindness* is providing as much detail as possible for your loved ones to plan the celebration of your life.

The average cost of a moderate funeral is between $7,000 and $10,000. Your funeral cost will be determined by the type of service you want. Make sure you have provided sufficient funds for the homegoing service of your choice through life insurance or a burial fund. You might want to visit a funeral home to get an estimate of the amount of money you will need for your service. Truthfully, it is the last party you will ever finance.

In addition to burial expenses, remember to provide for loss of income due to your death for minor children. Minor children are the remaining parent's responsibility until they become twenty-one.

What is the budget you want spent for your funeral? _____

Do you want to be cremated or buried? _____

If you want to be cremated:

Do you have a preference for your urn? If you have not given it much thought, take time to view options and not only gain an understanding of pricing, but write down your color and design preferences.

_____

_____

What would you like done with your ashes?

_____

_____

_____

If you want to be buried:

Do you have a casket preference? If you have not given it much thought, take some time to view casket options and not only gain an understanding of pricing, but write down your color and design preferences.

_____

_____

_____

Where do you want to be buried? What is your cemetery preference?

_____

_____

What do want to wear (list color(s), specific outfit/shoes, hairstyle, etc.)? Try to provide as much detail as possible. *While it is not required, if you have a very specific outfit in mind, leave the clothes, including underwear and shoes, in a labeled dress bag in your closet.*

_____

_____

_____

_____

Where do you want your funeral/homegoing service to be held?

_____

If applicable, who do you want to deliver your eulogy?

_____

What songs do you want sung? Who do you want to sing?

_____

_____

_____

_____

List any specific piece of text or scripture you want read.

_____

_____

If you want a repast and have preferences for the menu, list them here.

_____

_____

_____

_____

Finally, write your obituary. A sample outline is included in the SAMPLE TEMPLATES AND FORMS section.

_____

_____

_____

_____

_____

SAMPLE TEMPLATES AND FORMS

HEALTH CARE PROXY

(sample template)

I, _____ (your name) hereby appoint
_____ (appointee's name), residing
at: _____ (address) can be reached
at _____ (home phone number and/or cell number) as
my health care agent to make any and all health care decisions for me, except
to the extent that I state otherwise. This proxy shall take effect only when and
if I become unable to make my own health care decisions.

Optional: Alternate Agent
If the person I appoint is unable or unavailable to function as my health care
agent, I hereby appoint _____ (appointee's name),
residing at: _____ (address) can be reached
at _____ (home phone number and/or cell number) as my health
care agent to make any and l health care decisions for me, except to the extent
that I state otherwise. This proxy shall take effect only when and if I become
unable to make my own health care decisions.

Unless I revoke it or state an expiration date or circumstances under which it
will expire, this proxy shall remain in effect indefinitely. (Optional: If you want
this proxy to expire, state the date or conditions here.) This proxy shall expire
(specify date or conditions):

_____

(attach additional pages as necessary):

For your agent to make health care decisions for you about artificial nutrition
and hydration (nourishment and water provided by feeding tube and
intravenous line), your agent must know your wishes. You can either tell your
agent what your wishes are or include them in this section. See instructions for
sample language that you could use if you choose to include your wishes on
this form, including your wishes about artificial nutrition and hydration.

Your Identification (please print)

Your Name: _____

Your Signature: _____
Date: _____/_____/_____

Your Address: _____

_____

Optional: Organ and/or Tissue Donation
(Note: if you donate your body to science, your family has no control over how it will be used.)

I hereby make an anatomical gift, to be effective upon my death, of: (check any that apply)

☐ Any needed organs and/or tissues

☐ The following organs and/or tissues

_____

_____

☐ Limitations

_____

_____

If you do not state your wishes or instructions about organ and/or tissue donation on this form, it will not be taken to mean that you do not wish to donate or prevent a person, who is otherwise authorized by law, to consent to a donation on your behalf.

Your Signature _____ Date _____

Statement by Witnesses (Witnesses must be 18 years of age or older and cannot be the health care agent or alternate.)

I declare that the person who signed this document is personally known to me and appears to be of sound mind and acting of his or her own free will. He or she signed (or asked another to sign for him or her) this document in my presence.

Witness #1:

Date: _____/_____/_____

Name: _____ (print)

Signature: _____

Address: _____

_____

_____

Witness #2:

Date: _____/_____/_____

Name: _____ (print)

Signature: _____

Address: _____

_____

_____

LIVING WILL DECLARATION

(sample template)

I, _____(your name) of
_____(your address).

Being of sound mind, willfully and voluntarily make this declaration to be followed if I become incompetent or otherwise incapable of expressing my decision concerning my medical treatment. This declaration reflects my firm and settled commitment to refuse life-sustaining treatment under the circumstances indicated below.

I direct my attending physician, or whoever may be involved in such a decision, to withhold or withdraw life-sustaining treatment that serves only to prolong the process of my dying, if I should be in a terminal condition, a persistent vegetative state, irreversible coma or in a state of permanent unconsciousness.

Unless I indicate to the contrary in the paragraphs below, I direct that treatment be limited to measures to keep me comfortable and to relieve pain, including any pain that might occur by withholding or withdrawing life-sustaining treatment.

In addition, if I am in the condition described above, I hereby make the following advance directions about the following forms of treatment: that I want or do not want.

(Circle I do or I do not)

I DO/DO NOT want cardiac resuscitation or a cardiac pacemaker.

I DO/DO NOT want blood or blood products.

I DO/DO NOT want tube feeding or any other artificial or invasive form of nutrition (food) or hydration (water).

I DO/DO NOT want mechanical respiration.

I DO/DO NOT want kidney dialysis.

I DO/DO NOT want antibiotics.

I DO/DO NOT want any form of surgery or invasive diagnostic tests.

I DO/DO NOT want receipt of an organ.

I realize that if I do not specifically indicate my preference regarding any of the forms of treatment listed above, I may receive that form of treatment.

OTHER INSTRUCTIONS:

I DO/DO NOT want to designate another person as my surrogate to make medical treatment decisions for me if I should become incompetent and in a terminal condition or in a state of permanent unconsciousness.

Name of surrogate (if applicable):

The declarant or the person on behalf of and at the direction of the declarant knowingly and voluntarily signed this writing by signature or mark in my presence.

Declarant's signature _____

I made this declaration on the Declarant's address:

___ day of _____, 20___.

Witness' signature _____
Witness' address _____

Witness' signature _____
Witness' address _____

LAST WILL AND TESTAMENT

(sample template)

THIS IS THE LAST WILL AND TESTAMENT of _____, of New York, State of New York, made the year and date written below, hereby expressly revoking all my prior Wills and Codicils made at any time.

EXECUTOR AND TRUSTEE

I appoint _____, of New York, State of New York, to be the Executor and Trustee of my Will. If they do not survive me or are or become unwilling or unable to act as my Executor and Trustee before all the trusts set out in my Will have been fully performed, I appoint _____, residing in New York, State of New York, to be the Executors and Trustees of my Will. In my Will, I refer to the Executor and Trustee or Executors and Trustees, original or substituted or surviving, as my "Personal Representative."

CASH LEGACIES & OTHER SPECIFIC BEQUESTS

My Estate Trustee shall pay the following cash legacy(s) and transfer the following specific bequest(s) as soon as possible after my death: I leave _____ to the following: If _____pre-deceases me, I would like the primary beneficiary to be: _____

Contingent/Alternate Beneficiaries in case of the death of all the above: 100% in this order: _____

RESIDUE

If my primary beneficiary, _____, of New York, State of New York ("Primary Beneficiary"), is living on the thirtieth day following the date of my death, my Personal Representative shall pay and transfer the residue of my estate to them for their own use absolutely.

If my Primary Beneficiary is not living on the thirtieth day following the date of my death, my Estate Trustee shall pay and transfer the residue of my estate equally to my children. If a child has predeceased me leaving issue, then that child's share is to be paid and transferred to their issue equally. If all my children have predeceased me without issue, then my Estate Trustee shall pay and transfer the residue of my estate to _____ State of New York

IN TESTIMONY WHEREOF I have to my Will, which is written upon this and all preceding pages of paper, subscribed my name on this (date) day of (month), (year).

Signed,

SIGNED BY _____, as their Will, in the presence of us, present at the same time, who at their request, in their presence and in the presence of each other have subscribed our names as witnesses:

(Note: New York State requires a minimum of two witnesses. Obtain the requirements for your state of residence.)

Signature of Witness #1 _____

Print Name _____

Address _____

Phone _____

Occupation _____

Signature of Witness #2 _____

Print Name _____

Address _____

Phone _____

Occupation _____

DURABLE POWER OF ATTORNEY

(sample template)

NEW YORK STATUTORY SHORT FORM

THE POWERS YOU GRANT BELOW CONTINUE TO BE EFFECTIVE
SHOULD YOU BECOME DISABLED OR INCOMPETENT

DESIGNATION OF AGENT(S):

I, _____,

_____

(Your name and address above) Hereby appoint:

_____

(name(s) and address(es) of agent(s) above)

If you designate more than one agent above, they must act together unless you initial the statement below.

( ) My agents may act SEPARATELY.

( ) DESIGNATION OF SUCCESSOR AGENT(S): (OPTIONAL)
If every agent designated above is unable or unwilling to serve, I appoint as my successor agent(s):

_____

(name(s) and address(es) of successor agent(s))

Successor agents designated above must act together unless you initial the statement below.

( ) My successor agents may act SEPARATELY.

( ) This POWER OF ATTORNEY shall not be affected by my subsequent incapacity unless I have stated otherwise below, under "Modifications". (e) This POWER OF ATTORNEY REVOKES all prior Powers of Attorney executed by me unless I have stated otherwise below, under "Modifications."

If you are NOT revoking your prior Powers of Attorney, and if you are granting the same authority in two or more Powers of Attorney, you must also indicate under "Modifications" whether the agents given these powers are to act together or separately. *(If neither blank space is initialed, the agents will be required to act TOGETHER)*

IN MY NAME, PLACE AND STEAD, in any way which I myself could do, if I were personally present, with respect to the following matters as each of them is defined in Title 15 of Article 5 of the New York General Obligations Law to the extent that I am permitted by law to act through an agent:

DIRECTIONS: Initial in the blank space to the left of your choice any one or more of the following lettered subdivisions as to which you WANT to give your agent authority. If the blank space to the left of any lettered subdivision is NOT initialed, NO AUTHORITY WILL BE GRANTED for matters included in that subdivision.

Alternatively, the letter corresponding to each power you wish to grant may be written or typed on the blank line in subdivision "(Q)", and you may then put your initials in the blank space to the left of subdivision "(Q)" to grant each of the powers so indicated.)

[ ] (A) real estate transactions.
[ ] (B) chattel and goods transactions;
[ ] (C) bond, share and commodity transactions.
[ ] (D) banking transactions.
[ ] (E) business operating transactions.
[ ] (F) insurance transactions.
[ ] (G) estate transactions.
[ ] (H) claims and litigation;
[ ] (I) personal relationships and affairs.
[ ] (J) benefits from military service.
[ ] (K) records, reports, and statements.
[ ] (L) retirement benefit transactions;
[ ] (M) making gifts to my spouse, children and more remote descendants, and parents, not to exceed in the aggregate $10,000 to each of such persons in any year.

[ ] (N) tax matters;

[ ] (O) all other matters.

[ ] (P) full and unqualified authority to my attorney(s)-in-fact to delegate any or all the foregoing powers to any person or persons whom my attorney(s)-in-fact shall select.

[ ] (Q) each of the above matters identified by the following letters:

_____

(Special provisions and limitations may be included in the statutory short form durable power of attorney only if they conform to the requirements of 5-1503 of the New York General Obligations Law.)

This Durable Power of Attorney shall not be affected by my subsequent disability or incompetence.

If every agent named above is unable, or unwilling to serve, I appoint (insert name and address of successor) _____ to be my agent for all purposes here under.

To induce any third party to act hereunder, I hereby agree that any third party receiving a duly executed copy or facsimile of this instrument may act hereunder, and that revocation or termination hereof shall be ineffective as to such third party unless and until actual notice or knowledge of such revocation or termination shall have been received by such third party, and I for myself and for my heirs, executors, legal representatives and assigns, hereby agree to indemnify and hold harmless any such third party from and against any and all claims that may arise against such third party by reason of such third party having relied on the provisions of this instrument.

This Durable General Power of Attorney may be revoked by me at any time.

In Witness Whereof, I have hereunto signed my name this _____ day of _____, 20_____.

(YOU SIGN HERE:) _____ (Signature of Principal)

ACKNOWLEDGMENT
(for use within the State of New York)

STATE OF NEW YORK, COUNTY OF ss.:

On the day of in the year, 20__ before me, the undersigned, a Notary Public in and for said State, personally appeared personally known to me or proved to me on the basis of satisfactory evidence to be the individual(s) whose name is (are) subscribed to the within instrument and acknowledged to me that he/she/they executed the same in his/her/their capacity(ies), and that by his/her/their signature(s) on the instrument, the individual(s), or the person upon behalf of which the individual(s) acted, executed the instrument.

_____

Notary Public: State of New York

ACKNOWLEDGMENT
(for use outside the State of New York)

STATE OF, COUNTY OF ss.:

On the day of in the year, before me, the undersigned, a Notary Public in and for said State, personally appeared personally known to me or proved to me on the basis of satisfactory evidence to be the individual(s) whose name(s) is (are) subscribed to the within instrument and acknowledged to me that he/she/they executed the same in his/her/their capacity(ies), and that by his/her/their signature(s) on the instrument, the individual(s), or the person upon behalf of which the individual(s) acted, executed the instrument, and that such individual made such appearance before the undersigned in

(Insert city or political subdivision and state or county or other place acknowledgment taken).

_____

(Signature and office of individual taking acknowledgment)

NAME / ANNOUNCEMENT

Full name of the deceased, including nickname, if any

Age at death

Residence (for example, the name of the city) at death

Day and date of death (remember to include the year)

Place of death

Cause of death

LIFE

Date of birth

Place of birth

Names of parents

Childhood: siblings, stories, schools, friends

Marriage(s): date of, place, name of spouse

Education: school, college, university and other

Designations, awards, and other recognition

Employment: jobs, activities, stories, colleagues, satisfactions, promotions, union activities, frustrations,

Places of residence

Hobbies, sports, interests, activities, and other enjoyment

Charitable, religious, fraternal, political, and other affiliations; positions held

Achievements

Disappointments

Unusual attributes, humor, other stories

FAMILY

Survived by (and place of residence):

    Spouse

    Children (in order of date of birth, and their spouses)

    Grandchildren

    Great-grandchildren

    Great-great-grandchildren

    Parents

    Grandparents

Siblings (in order of date of birth)
Others, such as nephews, nieces, cousins, godchildren, in-laws
Friends
Pets (if appropriate)
Predeceased by (and date of death):
Spouse
Children (in order of date of birth)
Grandchildren
Siblings (in order of date of birth)
Others, such as nephews, nieces, cousins, godchildren, in-laws
Pets (if appropriate)

SERVICE

Day, date, time, place
Name of officiant, pallbearers, honorary pallbearers, other information
Visitation information if applicable: day, date, time, place
Reception information if applicable: day, date, time, place
Other memorial, vigil, or graveside services if applicable: day, date, time, place
Place of interment
Name of funeral home in charge of arrangements
Where to call for more information (even if no service planned)

Suggested details to include at the end of a funeral service, if applicable:

Memorial funds established
Memorial donation suggestions, including addresses
Thank you to people, groups, or institutions
Quotation or poem
Words to inspire living – request that family and friends state three words or more that sum up the life of the person who has transitioned.

You cannot go back to the past or predict the future. Enjoy the gift of life now. Live in your power of now. Don't have your last thoughts be "what if I had" or "I shoulda, woulda, coulda!" Don't let the champion in you be buried in the cemetery. Pursue your dreams. It takes one step to start a path. Start your path for a blessed life.

www.ingramcontent.com/pod-product-compliance
Lightning Source LLC
Chambersburg PA
CBHW081307140626
46546CB00022B/3449